SPELLING

YEAR 1

PASCAL PRESS

Reading Eggspress Spelling Workbook – Year 1

Reprinted 2016, 2017, 2020, 2022, 2024

ISBN: 978-1-74215-306-3

Distrbuted by:
Pascal Press
PO Box 250
Glebe NSW 2037

Ph: (02) 8585 4085
Fax: (02) 8585 4058

Email: info@blake.com.au
Website: www.blake.com.au

Publisher: Katy Pike
Series editor: Amy Russo
Editors: Laura Anderson, Stacey Belgre
Designed and typeset by The Modern Art Production Group
Printed in China by 1010 Printing International Ltd

CONTENTS

LESSONS		SAMPLE WORDS	PAGE
1.1	Alphabet	up, dog	2
1.2	Short vowels	am, sun	4
1.3	Long vowels	most, sky	6
1.4	a-e, e-e, i-e, o-e, u-e	bake, these, kite, spoke, fuse	8
1.5	Double consonants	fluff, grill, mess	10
1.6	ea and ee	read, feed	12
1.7	ea exceptions	head, health	14
1.8	nk sound	sunk, brink	16
1.9	ar, er, ir, ur	arm, verb, girl, curl	18
1.10	ch and tch	rich hatch	20
1.11	Plurals	dogs, buses	22
1.12	Hard k and hard c	kind, cat	24
1.13	oo and ou	roof, group	26
1.14	Ending: ve	eve, give	28
1.15	oa and ow	toad, slow	30
1.16	Ending: er	water, player	32
1.17	ay and ai	stay, paint	34
1.18	Hard and soft c	cold, mice	36
1.19	ou and ow	loud, brown	38
1.20	Endings: et, it, ot	bucket, visit, pilot	40
1.21	or and ore	horn, store	42
1.22	Suffix: ing	meeting, speeding	44
1.23	Ending: y	lazy, city	46
1.24	oy and oi	toy, boil	48
1.25	air, ear, are	fair, hear, spare	50
1.26	Suffix: ed	wished, parked	52
1.27	Ending: le	apple, jungle	54
1.28	ew and ue	new, blue	56
1.29	wh and ph	wheel, photo	58
1.30	Endings: en, on	seven, bacon	60
1.31	ie and igh	fried, light	62
1.32	Suffixes: er, est	nicer, tallest	64
1.33	au and aw	haul, crawl	66
1.34	Compound words	cupcake, sunshine	68
1.35	Tricky words	was, your	70
1.36	Prefix: un	unpack, unclear	72
Rules and generalisations			74

WHAT IS READING EGGSPRESS?

Reading Eggspress is an online program designed to build language and literacy skills for students in Years 1–6. The program has targeted lesson sequences for Comprehension and Spelling that align with national curriculum standards for achievement. With built-in rewards, access to over 4000 e-books and rich assessment data to track progress, the Reading Eggspress program individualises learning to help students achieve their personal best.

How does the Reading Eggspress Spelling Program work?

Research proves that students have more spelling success if they learn to recognise common spelling patterns and generalisations as part of an explicit and systematic teaching program. The *Reading Eggspress Spelling program* focuses on common spelling rules, generalisations and strategies using a combination of teaching videos, engaging online activities, games and tests with fully integrated student books.

The *Reading Eggspress Spelling books* for Years 1–6 extend students as they learn, use and apply their spelling skills across a range of written activities. The student books work alongside the online program to reinforce learning for each lesson.

The *Reading Eggspress Spelling program* is structured to provide instruction on a spelling rule, strategy or generalisation with 36 lessons per year level. Each lesson is centred on a carefully crafted word list, based around the sound, structure or meaning features of words. These word lists have been created by consulting educational research and the Australian Curriculum.

Self-paced systematic program

Easy to understand videos

Assessment and instant feedback

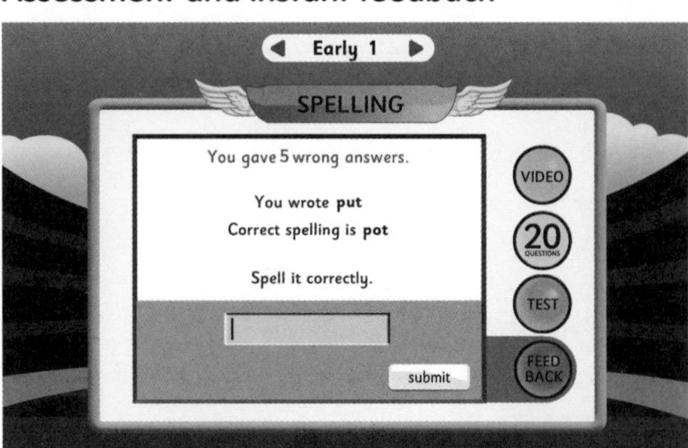

Practice activities

Reading Eggspress Spelling and the Australian Curriculum

Each lesson focuses on a core set of 20 words and 10 challenge words to extend students. These lists have been created to align with the Australian Curriculum Content Descriptions and Elaborations.

Year 1 Language

Expressing and developing ideas

ACELA1778

Know that regular one-syllable words are made up of letters and common letter clusters that correspond to the sounds heard, and how to use visual memory to write high-frequency word

- writing one-syllable words containing known blends, for example 'bl', 'st'

ACELA1455

Recognise and know how to use morphemes in word families for example 'play' in 'played' and 'playing'

- building word families from common morphemes (for example 'play', 'plays', 'playing', 'played', 'playground')
- using morphemes to read words (for example by recognising the 'stem' in words such as 'walk/ed')

Sound and letter knowledge

ACELA1458

Recognise sound-letter matches including common vowel and consonant digraphs and consonant blends

ACELA1459

Understand the variability of sound-letter matches

- recognising that letters can have more than one sound for example 'u' in 'cut', 'put', 'use' and 'a' in 'cat', 'father', 'any'
- recognising sounds that can be produced by different letters (for example the /s/ sound in 'sat', 'cent', 'scene')

Reading Eggspress Spelling

Each lesson uses a combination of activities from the following categories:

Proofreading: self-directed checking of written text. Proofreading assists the development of reading and writing.

Visual memory: the Look-say-cover-write-check creates a visual memory of the word. It is important as a self-correction skill.

Definitions: morphemic understanding of words. This skill is used selectively where an understanding of the etymology and morphological structure benefits orthographic understanding.

Word families: groups of words that share common morphemes. Identifying visual and morphemic commonalities aids accurate spelling and is used throughout the program.

Word sorts: groups of words that share a common theme. Word sorts have been integrated as grouping together like ideas helps learners make sense of the world around them.

Overview of Spelling Aspects Covered in Year 1

Spelling Aspect	Areas Covered	Pages
Digraphs and trigraphs	a-e, e-e, i-e, o-e, u-e; ea, ee; ar, er, ir, ur; oo, ou; oa, ow; ay, ai; ou, ow; or, ore; oy, oi; air, ear, are; ew, ue; wh, ph; ie, igh; au, aw	8, 9, 12, 13, 18, 19, 26, 27, 30, 31, 34, 35, 38, 39, 42, 43, 48, 49, 50, 51, 56, 57, 58, 59, 62, 63, 66, 67
Endings	double consonants; ve; er; et, it, ot; y; le; en, on	10, 11, 28, 29, 32, 33, 40, 41, 46, 47, 54, 55, 60, 61
Prefixes	un	72, 73
Suffixes	s, es; ing; ed; er, est	22, 23, 44, 45, 52, 53, 64, 65
Letter patterns	nk; ch, tch	16, 17, 20, 21
Other aspects of spelling	vowels and consonants; short vowels, long vowels; ea exceptions; hard k; hard and soft c; compound words; tricky words	2, 3, 4, 5, 6, 7, 14, 15, 24, 25, 36, 37, 68, 69, 70, 71

MY PROGRESS CHART • LESSONS 1.1 – 1.18

Name ______________________________

Lesson	Level	Online test score	Pages	Self-assessment *With this list I feel ...*
1.1 Alphabet		/10	2 - 3	
1.2 Short vowels		/10	4 - 5	
1.3 Long vowels		/10	6 - 7	
1.4 a-e, e-e, i-e, o-e, u-e		/10	8 - 9	
1.5 Double consonants		/10	10 - 11	
1.6 ea and ee		/10	12 - 13	
1.7 ea exceptions		/10	14 - 15	
1.8 nk sound		/10	16 - 17	
1.9 ar, er, ir, ur		/10	18 - 19	
1.10 ch and tch		/10	20 - 21	
1.11 Plurals		/10	22 - 23	
1.12 Hard k and hard c		/10	24 - 25	
1.13 oo and ou		/10	26 - 27	
1.14 Ending: ve		/10	28 - 29	
1.15 oa and ow		/10	30 - 31	
1.16 Ending: er		/10	32 - 33	
1.17 ay and ai		/10	34 - 35	
1.18 Hard and soft c		/10	36 - 37	

MY PROGRESS CHART • LESSONS 1.19 – 1.36

Name ____

Lesson	Level	Online test score	Pages	Self-assessment *With this list I feel ...*
1.19 ou and ow		/10	38 - 39	
1.20 Endings: et, it, ot		/10	40 - 41	
1.21 or and ore		/10	42 - 43	
1.22 Suffix: ing		/10	44 - 45	
1.23 Ending: y		/10	46 - 47	
1.24 oy and oi		/10	48 - 49	
1.25 air, ear, are		/10	50 - 51	
1.26 Suffix: ed		/10	52 - 53	
1.27 Ending: le		/10	54 - 55	
1.28 ew and ue		/10	56 - 57	
1.29 wh and ph		/10	58 - 59	
1.30 Endings: en, on		/10	60 - 61	
1.31 ie and igh		/10	62 - 63	
1.32 Suffixes: er, est		/10	64 - 65	
1.33 au and aw		/10	66 - 67	
1.34 Compound words		/10	68 - 69	
1.35 Tricky words		/10	70 - 71	
1.36 Prefix: un		/10	72 - 73	

Vowels and consonants

1 Copy each list word.

at ______	as ______	can ______	top ______
in ______	us ______	run ______	red ______
on ______	an ______	and ______	dog ______
up ______	if ______	sun ______	men ______
it ______	am ______	big ______	but ______

2 Name the picture. Write the word.

r ______

s ______

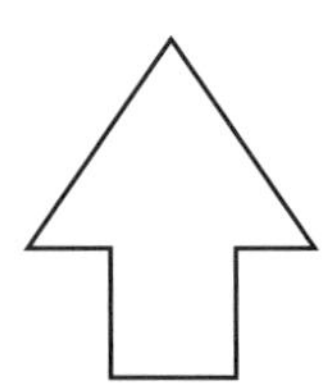

o ______

u ______

3 Opposites. Find the opposite.

down ______ small ______ bottom ______

off ______ out ______ moon ______

Vowels and consonants

Challenge words

4 Copy each challenge word.

cut ______________

yet ______________

zip ______________

win ______________

yes ______________

set ______________

end ______________

egg ______________

add ______________

lots ______________

5 Fill in the missing vowel.

y___t

___dd

s___t

z___p

w___n

l___ts

y___s

___gg

c___t

___nd

6 Complete the sentence.

I ______________ the paper.

The hen laid an ______________.

I nod and say ______________.

There was ______________ of food.

I can ______________ two and two.

My bag has a ______________.

She will ______________ the race.

Short vowels

1 Copy each list word.

on ________	in ________	sit ________	pot ________
up ________	am ________	fog ________	bed ________
at ________	dog ________	lid ________	sat ________
it ________	map ________	bad ________	wet ________
us ________	red ________	sun ________	man ________

2 Fill in the missing letters.

I look ____p and see the s____n.

The f____g is b____d today.

I found the town ____n the m____p.

The d____g ran to ____s.

The l____d is ____n the cupboard.

We found ____t ____t the park.

I ____m going to s____t on the r____d chair.

3 Name the picture. Write the word.

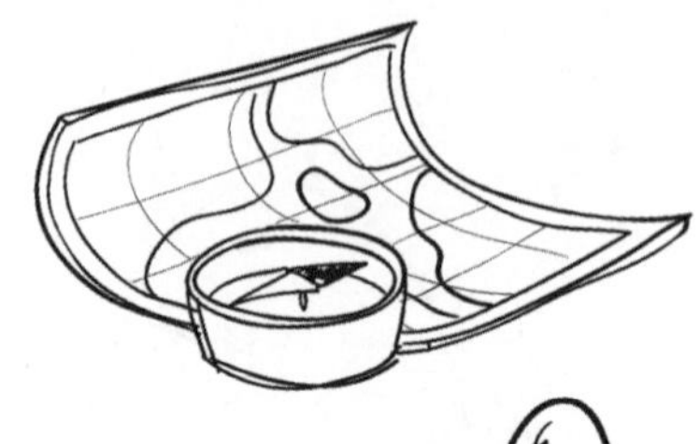

m ________

u ________

d ________

o ________

Challenge words

4 Copy each challenge word.

let ______	rug ______	bag ______
cut ______	hum ______	act ______
dot ______	hid ______	
hut ______	ran ______	

5 Fill in the missing letters.

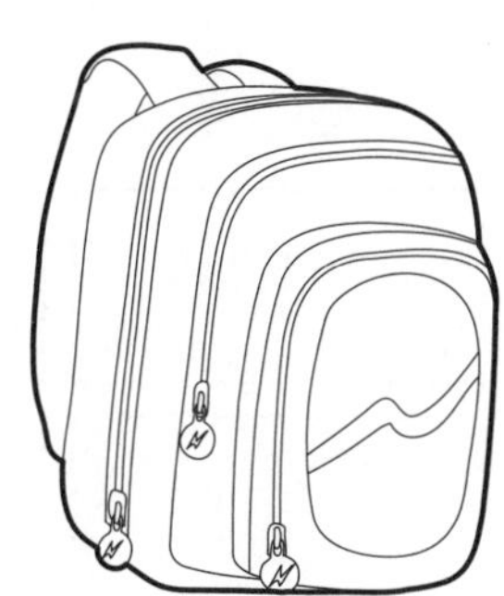

I l___ ___ her c___ ___ the ribbon.

I h___ ___ the gift in my b___ ___ .

The r___ ___ was inside the h___ ___.

6 Match the word to its meaning.

bag	to slice with something sharp
dot	a little mark or spot
act	something that is done
cut	you put things in me

Long vowels

1 Copy each list word.

no ______	by ______	dry ______	spy ______
be ______	go ______	try ______	fry ______
so ______	my ______	sky ______	most ______
me ______	he ______	cry ______	find ______
we ______	she ______	fly ______	why ______

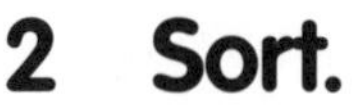

2 Sort.

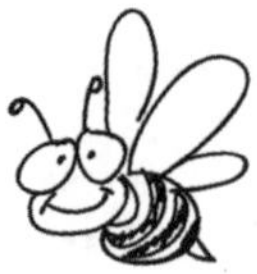

o	e	i	y	

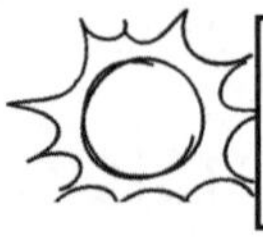

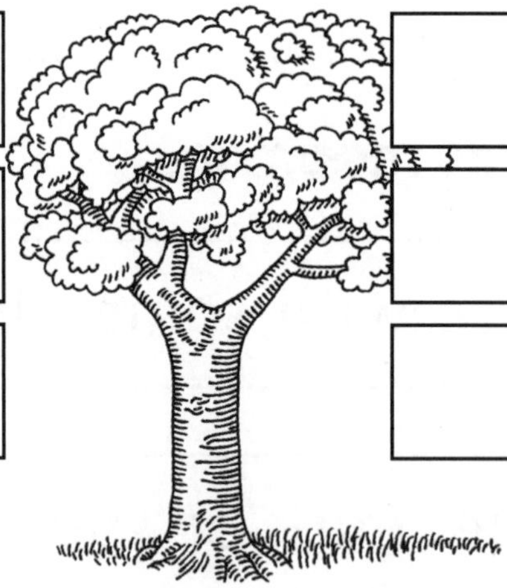

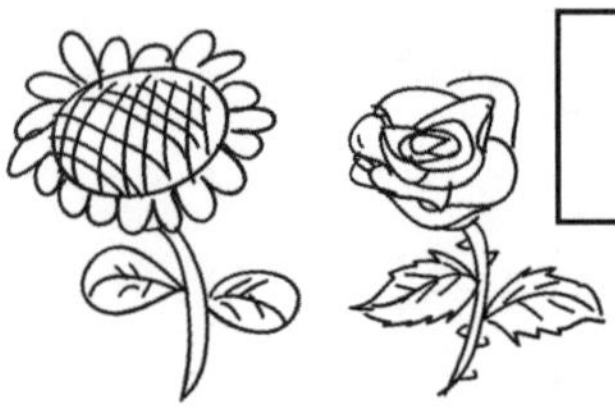

3 Make a list word by colouring the blocks.

mo	st / nd	w	hy / nd	fi	nd / ld

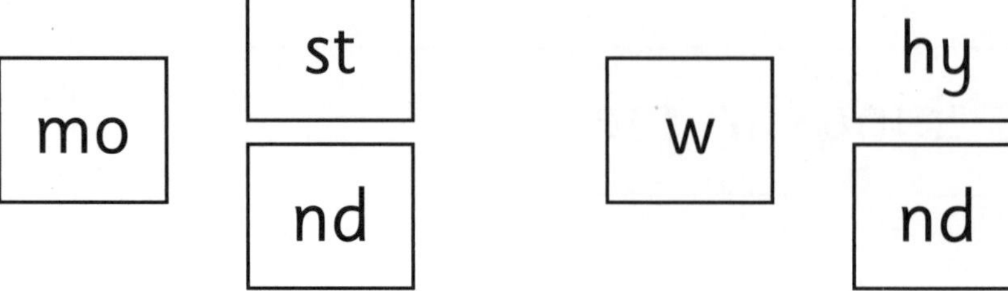

Long vowels

Challenge words

4 Copy each challenge word.

kind ______________

wild ______________

bind ______________

post ______________

rind ______________

child ______________

wind ______________

mind ______________

grind ______________

blind ______________

5 Fit the challenge words into their word shape.

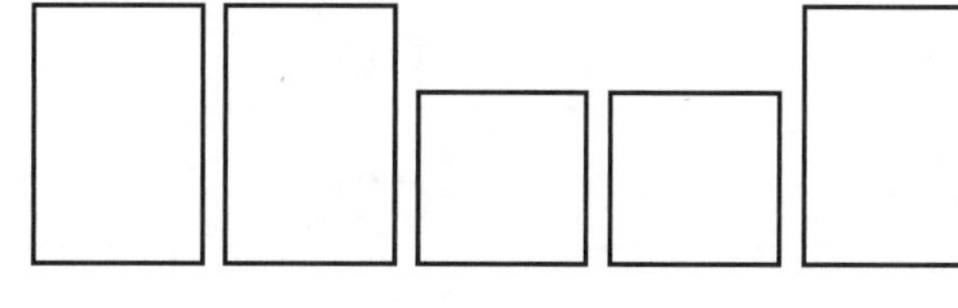

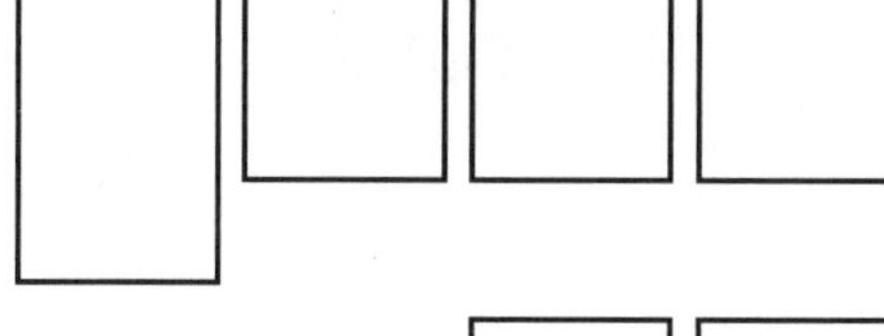

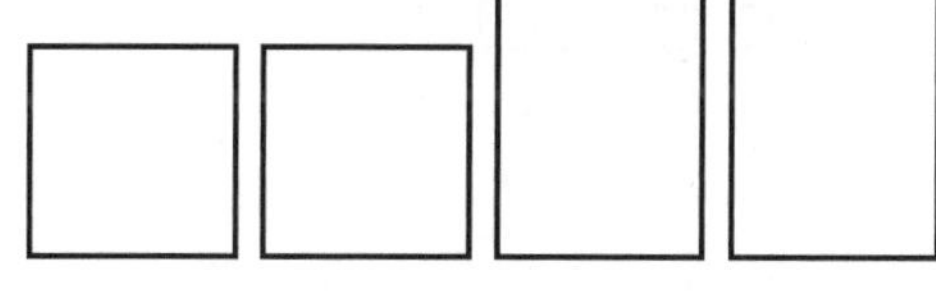

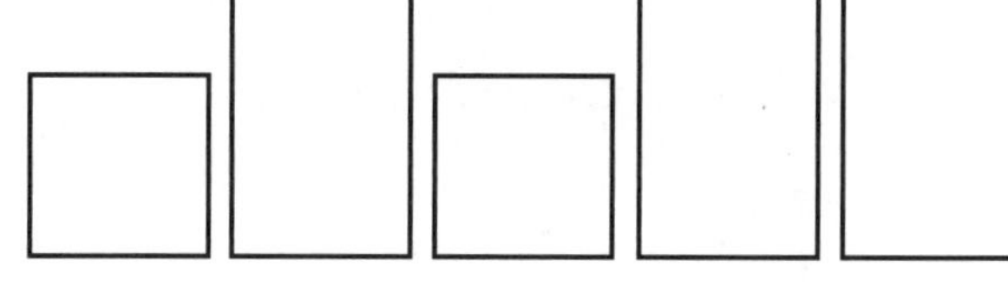

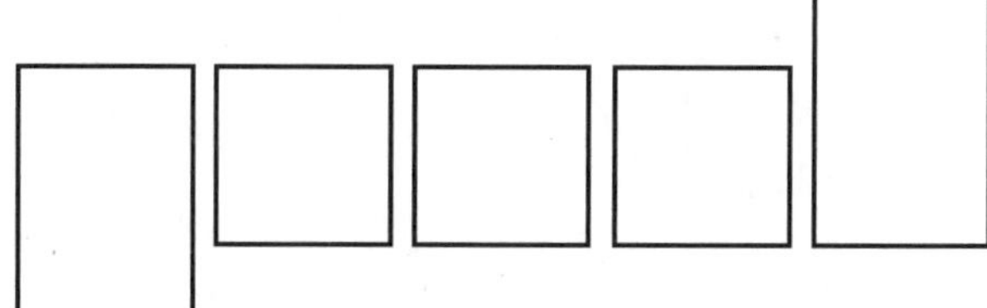

6 Complete the sentence using a challenge word.

The boy was nice and ______________.

The letter came in the ______________.

A wombat is a ______________ animal.

You can't eat the ______________ of a lime.

The ______________ liked her toy.

You ______________ the old clock to make it work.

Split digraphs – a-e, e-e, i-e, o-e, u-e

1 Copy each list word.

bake ________	bite ________	rule ________	those ________
five ________	mole ________	close ________	cone ________
hole ________	late ________	snake ________	cube ________
cute ________	kite ________	flame ________	pole ________
came ________	rose ________	these ________	tune ________

2 Label the picture.

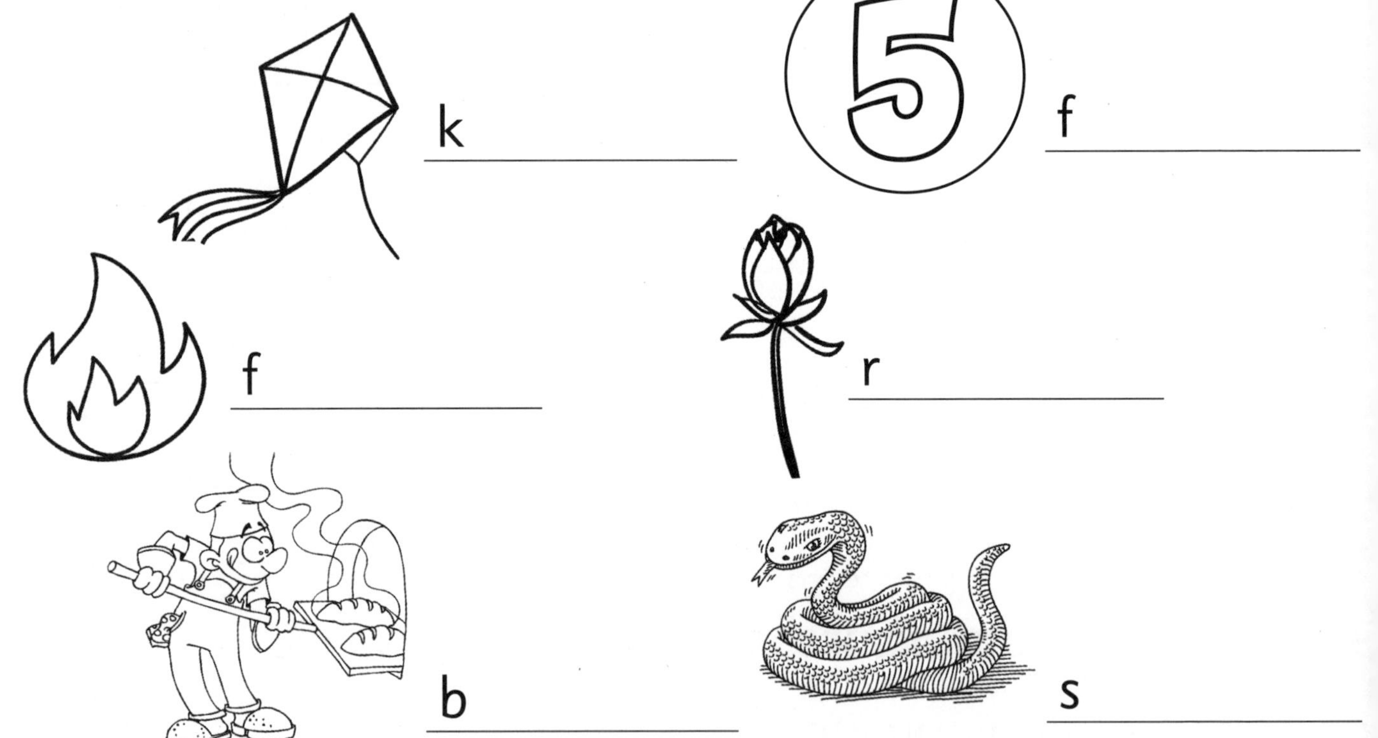

k ________

f ________

f ________

r ________

b ________

s ________

3 Fill in the missing vowel.

cl ____ se	c ____ me	h ____ le
l ____ te	c ____ be	m ____ le
c ____ te	b ____ ke	r ____ le

Challenge words

4 Copy each challenge word.

froze ______	spade ______	awake ______
theme ______	blaze ______	amaze ______
chose ______	slime ______	
spoke ______	flake ______	

5 Put each challenge word on the correct train.

6 Choose it. Circle and rewrite the correct word to complete the sentence.

I dug with a [spade] [spayd] . ______

The lake [frose] [froze] in winter. ______

He [choze] [chose] to eat an apple. ______

She was still [awake] [awaik] late at night. ______

Word endings – double consonants

1 Copy each list word.

will ______	smell ______	boss ______
fell ______	sell ______	cross ______
hill ______	doll ______	spill ______
less ______	puff ______	grill ______
dress ______	fuss ______	pill ______
mess ______	frill ______	press ______
bell ______	still ______	

2 Unscramble each word.

ff p u ______	e s ll ______
o ss b ______	ss e l ______
i ll w ______	e ll sm ______
u ss f ______	ll fr i ______
ll i st ______	e ss m ______

3 Name the picture. Write the word.

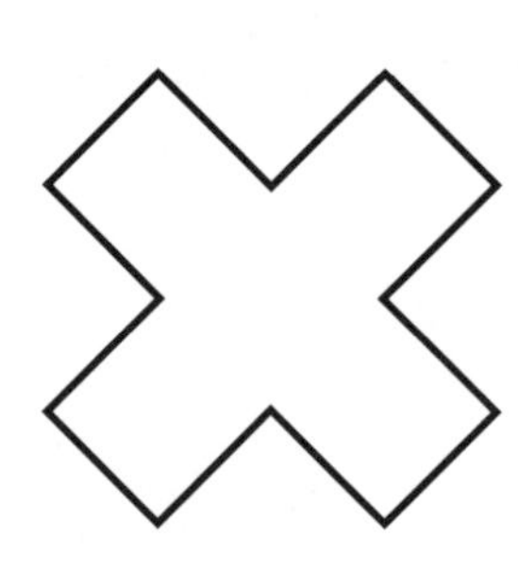

c ______

d ______

d ______

Word endings – double consonants

Challenge words

4 Copy each challenge word.

drill ____________ bliss ____________ floss ____________
skull ____________ cliff ____________ stiff ____________
gruff ____________ bluff ____________
fluff ____________ skill ____________

5 Choose it. Circle and rewrite the correct word to complete the sentence.

Dad says 'no' but he likes to [bluuf] [bluff].
____

Eating the ice-cream filled Sam with [bliss] [blis].
____

My mum will [flos] [floss] her teeth each night.
____

There was some [fluf] [fluff] on my sleeve.
____

6 Word clues. Which challenge word matches?

high place with a steep drop ____________
hard to bend ____________
the bones of the head ____________
a tool ____________
something you do well ____________

Vowel digraphs – ee, ea

1 Copy each list word.

eel ________	seen ________	each ________
bee ________	keep ________	cheat ________
feet ________	heat ________	cream ________
meat ________	teeth ________	beach ________
feed ________	green ________	clean ________
free ________	bleed ________	dream ________
read ________	cheek ________	

2 Name the picture. Write the word.

b ________

m ________

t ________

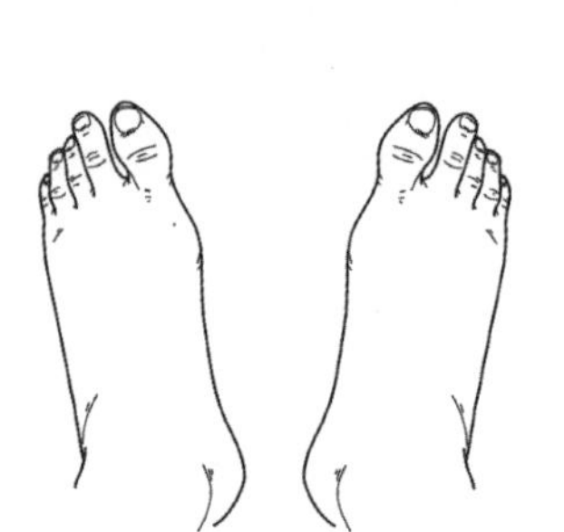

f ________

r ________

3 Fill in the missing letters.

ch ___ ___ k	bl ___ ___ d	s ___ ___ n
gr ___ ___ n	___ ___ ch	h ___ ___ t
f ___ ___ d	t ___ ___ th	d ___ ___ a ___
k ___ ___ p	fr ___ ___	c ___ e ___ m

Vowel digraphs – ee, ea

Challenge words

4 Copy each challenge word.

sheep	______	leash	______
peach	______	asleep	______
east	______	speed	______
agree	______	three	______
repeat	______	feast	______

5 Interesting question. Answer the question with a challenge word.

What means going fast? ______

What is a woolly animal? ______

Which word means *a large meal*? ______

What fruit has a thin, furry skin? ______

Which word is a number? ______

What means to do over and over? ______

6 Hidden words. Find the challenge word.

sdaeastshia ______

sseasleepeelh ______

aspleasheahb ______

azsloagreeipq ______

rpspeachqlt ______

Vowel digraphs – ea exceptions

1 Copy each list word.

bread ______	head ______
meant ______	ahead ______
read ______	heading ______
deaf ______	header ______
deadly ______	threat ______
lead ______	already ______
ready ______	thread ______
breath ______	health ______
heavy ______	healthy ______
instead ______	dealt ______

2 Unscramble each word.

ea r d y ______	l d ea ______
h d ea a ______	st d in ea ______
ea th d r ______	ea r t th ______
f d ea ______	r d ea ______
ea t n m ______	d d ea ly ______

3 Name the picture. Write the word.

h ______

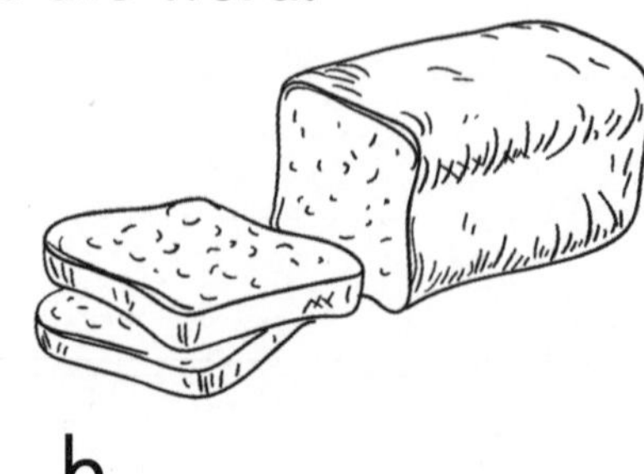

b ______

h ______

Vowel digraphs – ea exceptions

Challenge words

4 Copy each challenge word.

meadow	______	weather	______
dreamt	______	measure	______
steady	______	treasure	______
feather	______	heavens	______
leather	______	jealous	______

5 Choose it. Circle and rewrite the correct word to complete the sentence.

The [weather] [wether] is fine today. ______

Mum [measores] [measures] with a ruler. ______

I found the [feather] [fether] on the ground. ______

Jack [dremt] [dreamt] that he was flying. ______

6 Silly sentences. Use as many challenge words as possible to make a silly story.

______

______

______

______

nk sound

1 Copy each list word.

bank	______	rink	______	stink	______
link	______	sunk	______	plank	______
pink	______	wink	______	drank	______
sink	______	junk	______	stank	______
tank	______	blank	______	trunk	______
bunk	______	blink	______	yank	______
honk	______	drink	______		

2 Unscramble each word.

nk a t	______	u nk s	______
a l b nk	______	nk p i	______
o nk h	______	r nk a	______
r a nk d	______	u nk j	______

3 Name the picture. Write the word.

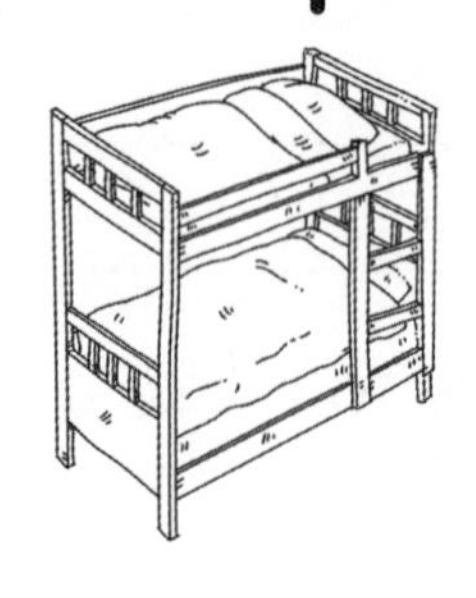

b ______

s ______

d ______

w ______

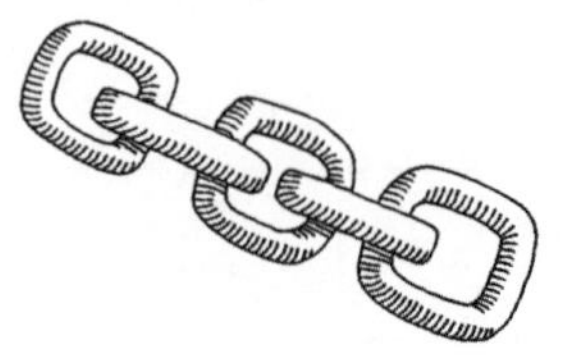

l ______

Challenge words

4 Copy each challenge word.

clink	______	chink	______
prank	______	oink	______
skunk	______	chunk	______
think	______	shrink	______
thank	______	shrunk	______

5 Interesting question. Answer the question with a challenge word.

What is the sound a pig makes? ______

Which word is a type of animal? ______

What do you do with your brain? ______

What should you do when someone helps you? ______

6 Acrostic poem. Use the word **clink** to write an acrostic poem.

C ______

L ______

I ______

N ______

K ______

Vowel digraphs – ar, er, ir, ur

1 Copy each list word.

arm	______	cart	______	march	______
are	______	girl	______	dirt	______
car	______	bird	______	hurt	______
park	______	arch	______	farm	______
her	______	stir	______	star	______
far	______	skirt	______	paper	______
fur	______	turn	______		

2 Label. Use a list word.

c ______

b ______

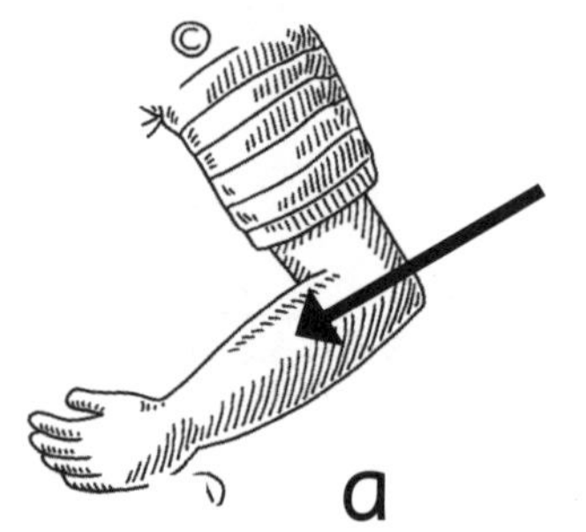

a ______

3 Write the words on the correct cars.

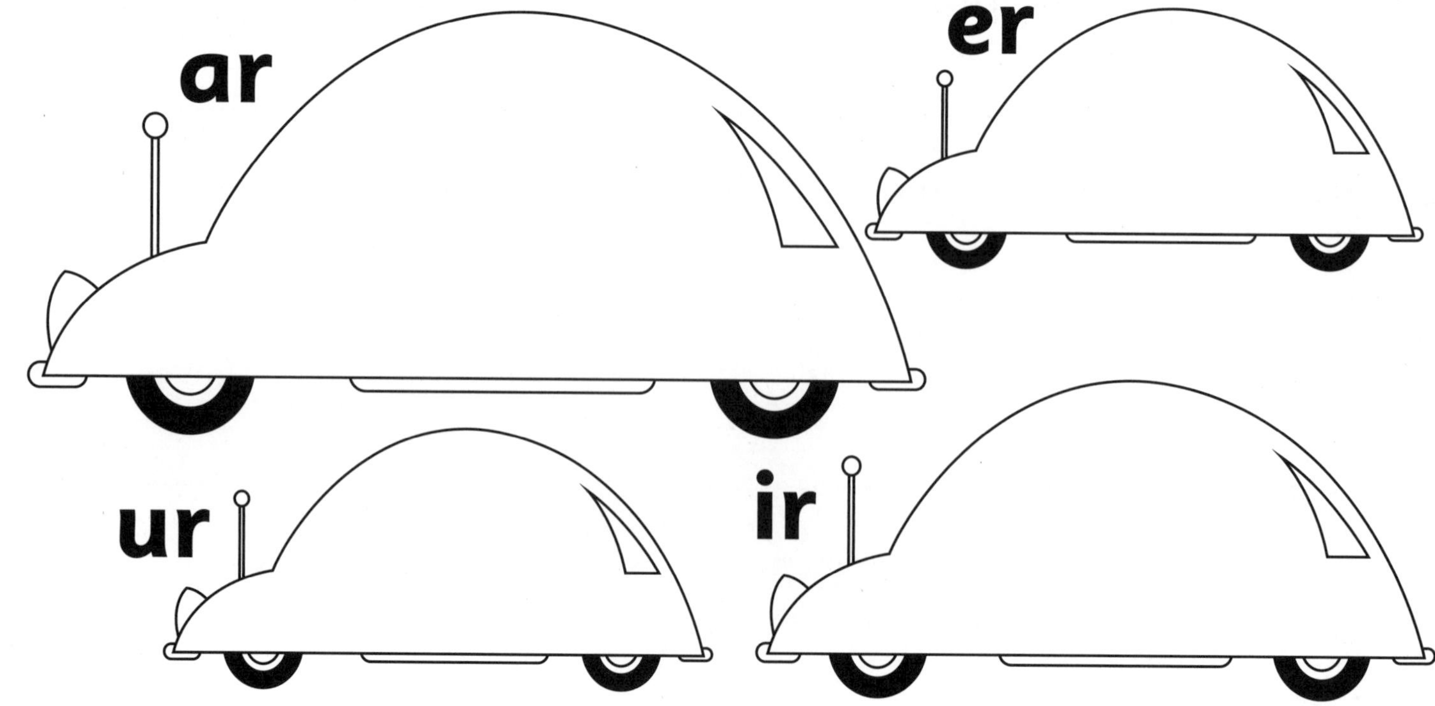

Vowel digraphs – ar, er, ir, ur

Challenge words

4 Copy each challenge word.

garden ____________	smart ____________
person ____________	third ____________
Thursday ____________	start ____________
thirty ____________	burst ____________
first ____________	nurse ____________

5 Word clues. Which challenge word matches?

weekday ____________

to begin ____________

grass and flowers ____________

medical carer ____________

one more than 29 ____________

clever ____________

6 Hidden words. Find the challenge word.

asdburstiah ____________

qftpersonasu ____________

asrthirdasin ____________

padstartasdu ____________

Consonant digraphs and trigraphs – ch, tch 1.10

1 Copy each list word.

much	____________	hatch	____________	latch	____________
such	____________	patch	____________	which	____________
itch	____________	batch	____________	watch	____________
rich	____________	pinch	____________	clutch	____________
catch	____________	hutch	____________	ditch	____________
each	____________	peach	____________	branch	____________
fetch	____________	bench	____________		

2 **Label.** Use a list word.

b____________ p____________ b____________ w____________

3 **Rainbow write.** Write the list words in different colours.

Consonant digraphs and trigraphs – ch, tch

Challenge words

4 Copy each challenge word.

speech	______	stretch	______
switch	______	march	______
sketch	______	torch	______
stitch	______	kitchen	______
scratch	______	butcher	______

5 Solve it. Read the clue and complete the sentence.

What is a type of fast walking? ______

What do you do when you have an itch? ______

What room are meals cooked in? ______

Who sells meat? ______

What do you use to turn the light on? ______

What is a type of drawing? ______

6 Choose it. Circle and rewrite the correct word to complete the sentence.

I always [strech] [stretch] before I run. ______

I wrote a [speech] [speche] about tigers. ______

I used the [tauch] [torch] to see in the dark. ______

Making plurals – adding s and es

1 Copy each list word.

dogs ____________	boxes ____________	lunches ____________
buses ____________	shops ____________	beaches ____________
boats ____________	socks ____________	snakes ____________
zoos ____________	wishes ____________	riches ____________
frogs ____________	peaches ____________	brushes ____________
bikes ____________	clocks ____________	plates ____________
eggs ____________	grapes ____________	

2 More than one. Write the single word and the plural word.

Making plurals – adding s and es

Challenge words

3 Copy each challenge word.

bushes	______	dresses	______
torches	______	glasses	______
benches	______	patches	______
gloves	______	towers	______
coaches	______	churches	______

4 Choose it. Circle and rewrite the word to complete the sentence.

I wore my [glovs] [gloves] . ______

The cat hid in the [bushes] [bushs] . ______

Mum wears [glasses] [glases] to read. ______

The [towas] [towers] were tall. ______

They used [torchs] [torches] to see in the dark. ______

The twins wore matching [dresses] [dreses] . ______

5 Solve it. Read the clue and complete the sentence.

You put us on torn clothes. We are ______ .

You sit on us to wait for the bus. We are ______ .

You wear us to help you see. We are ______ .

We are green and leafy. We are ______ .

Hard k sounds

1 Copy each list word.

act ______	skin ______	kept ______
kiss ______	curl ______	skill ______
cone ______	cash ______	snake ______
cool ______	clash ______	scrape ______
keep ______	come ______	husky ______
kind ______	keen ______	coal ______
card ______	donkey ______	

2 Sort the words.

Words with the letter **c**.

Words with the letter **k**.

3 **Unscramble it.** Unscramble the letters to make a list word.

pecrsa ______ hcsa ______

eekp ______ liksl ______

Hard k sounds

Challenge words

4 Copy each challenge word.

cheeky	____________	awoke	____________
sneaky	____________	crayon	____________
kitten	____________	cabin	____________
biscuit	____________	castle	____________
kettle	____________	monkey	____________

5 Hidden words. Find the challenge word.

asdcrayonasdy ____________

asjfmonkeyasdy ____________

wahdawokeasd ____________

sdfbcastlezsd ____________

cwplcabinasdu ____________

vsdfgkettleasd ____________

6 Match the clue to a challenge word.

1.			s				
2.				i		▨	▨
3.		i					▨
4.		h					▨
5.					k		▨

1. something you eat
2. a room on a ship
3. a young cat
4. rude or annoying
5. acting in a secret way

Vowel digraphs – oo and ou

1 Copy each list word.

too ______	roof ______	tooth ______
zoo ______	food ______	soup ______
you ______	cook ______	stool ______
book ______	hood ______	mood ______
moon ______	boot ______	shook ______
good ______	bloom ______	droop ______
look ______	broom ______	

2 Fill in the missing words.

I am ______ at maths.
The ______ shines at night.
I have read that ______ .
I saw an elephant at the ______ .
I love a hot bowl of ______ .
He was in a bad ______ .

3 Rhyming words. Choose a list word that rhymes with the word.

zoo ______
book ______
bloom ______
food ______
good ______

Vowel digraphs – oo and ou

Challenge words

4 Copy each challenge word.

swoop	____________	raccoon	____________
group	____________	hooray	____________
spoon	____________	balloon	____________
goose	____________	bamboo	____________
choose	____________	baboon	____________

5 Solve it. Read the clue and complete the sentence.

You can blow me up. I am a ____________.

You can use me to eat with. I am a ____________.

I lay eggs and swim in the water. I am a ____________.

I am a large monkey. I am a ____________.

I am something a bird does. I am ____________.

Pandas eat me. I am ____________.

6 Hidden words. Find the challenge word.

aujerraccoonhayj ____________

grplgroupasi ____________

asdechoosehalh ____________

asdhoorayasui ____________

blkballoonklnbl ____________

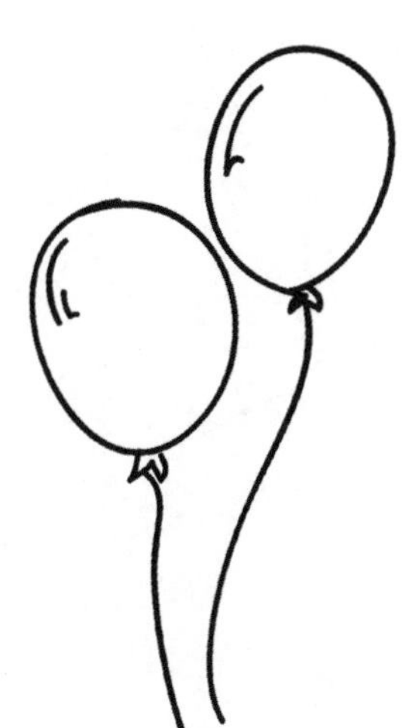

Word endings – ve

1 Copy each list word.

eve	__________	glove	__________	improve	__________
have	__________	nerve	__________	remove	__________
live	__________	dove	__________	valve	__________
love	__________	above	__________	curve	__________
move	__________	carve	__________	active	__________
leave	__________	twelve	__________	sleeve	__________
serve	__________	prove	__________		

2 Write the list words in alphabetical order.

__________	__________	__________	__________
__________	__________	__________	__________
__________	__________	__________	__________
__________	__________	__________	__________
__________	__________	__________	__________

3 Name the picture. Use a list word.

g __________

l __________

t __________

s __________

d __________

a __________

Word endings – ve

Challenge words

4 Copy each challenge word.

olive ______	swerve ______
solve ______	massive ______
shove ______	believe ______
halve ______	arrive ______
starve ______	forgive ______

5 Choose it. Circle and rewrite the correct word to complete the sentence.

The new building is [massive] [masiv]. ______

I ate the [oliv] [olive]. ______

I will [forgiv] [forgive] my brother. ______

He will [solv] [solve] the crime. ______

We had to [swerv] [swerve] to miss the bird. ______

She will [halve] [halv] the apple and share it. ______

6 Words within words. Can you rearrange the letters in **massive** to make 6 new words?

______ ______

______ ______

______ ______

Vowel digraphs – oa and ow

1 Copy each list word.

oak	______	soap	______	show	______
bow	______	coat	______	owe	______
row	______	toad	______	slow	______
oats	______	crow	______	own	______
low	______	soak	______	cloak	______
boat	______	glow	______	bowl	______
road	______	moan	______		

2 Sort the words.

oa		ow	

3 Correct it. Rewrite the misspelled word with the correct spelling.

We went sailing on the bote. ______

Mum tied a bo in my hair. ______

The bole was full of berries. ______

We had to roe the boat to shore. ______

The lights made the tree gloe. ______

Vowel digraphs – oa and ow

Challenge words

4 Copy each challenge word.

blown ____________ boast ____________

groan ____________ croak ____________

grown ____________ roast ____________

coast ____________ elbow ____________

coach ____________ below ____________

5 Complete the sentence.

We had ____________ potatoes for dinner.

My ____________ is part of my arm.

I have ____________ taller.

I watched the people walking ____________.

The leaves had ____________ all over the yard.

The frog makes a noise that sounds like ____________.

6 Acrostic poem. Use the word **coast** to write an acrostic poem.

C ____________

O ____________

A ____________

S ____________

T ____________

Word endings – er

1 Copy each list word.

ever	______	finger	______	corner	______
under	______	sister	______	clever	______
never	______	mother	______	flower	______
enter	______	other	______	father	______
water	______	teacher	______	gather	______
silver	______	wonder	______	counter	______
winter	______	player	______		

2 **Addition words.** Add the two parts to make the word.

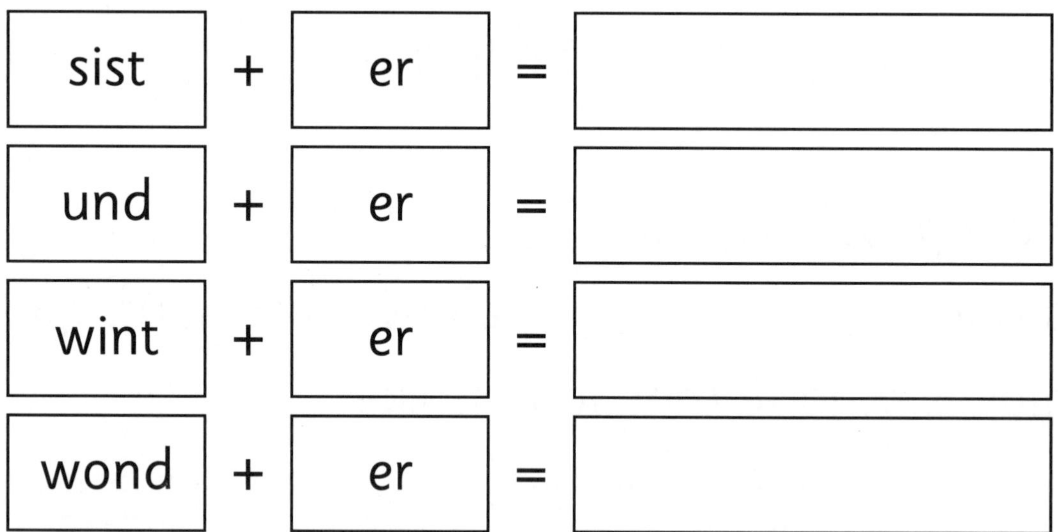

sist	+	er	=	
und	+	er	=	
wint	+	er	=	
wond	+	er	=	

3 **Label it.** Use a list word.

f ______

m ______

w ______

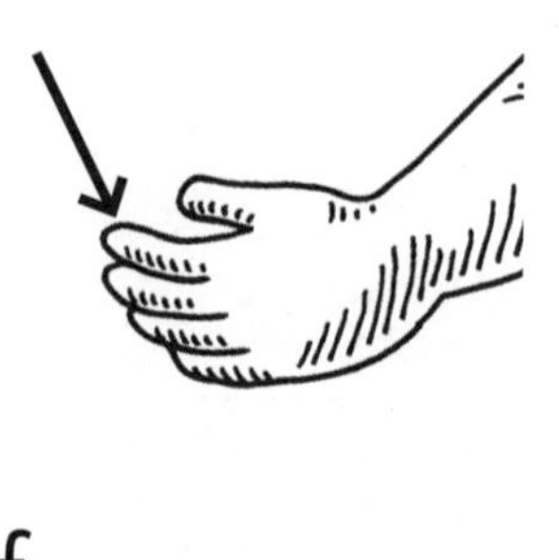

f ______

Word endings – er

Challenge words

4 Copy each challenge word.

cover ______	swimmer ______
brother ______	butter ______
monster ______	ladder ______
letter ______	winner ______
matter ______	together ______

5 Choose it. Circle and rewrite the correct word to complete the sentence.

I [cova] [cover] my mouth if I sneeze. ______

Grandma sent me a [letter] [leter] . ______

He climbed up the [lader] [ladder] . ______

We go to school [togetha] [together] . ______

She likes [butter] [butta] on her bread. ______

She is a great [swimer] [swimmer] . ______

6 Hidden words. Find the challenge word.

gflmatterash ______

qplcmonsterkhyw ______

stlebrothermalo ______

whkwinnernldw ______

Vowel digraphs – ay, ai

1 Copy each list word.

say	stay	claim
day	sail	brain
aim	pain	sway
may	tail	grain
play	plain	paint
main	snail	stain
rain	chain	

2 Sort the words.

ay **ai**

3 Rhyming words. Choose a list word that rhymes.

plain

sway

tail

Vowel digraphs – ay, ai

Challenge words

4 Copy each challenge word.

again	______	stray	______
away	______	faint	______
braid	______	spray	______
waist	______	sprain	______
today	______	always	______

5 Interesting question. Answer these questions using the challenge words.

What can you do with your hair? ______

What is a part of your body? ______

What is another word for repeat? ______

What day is it right now? ______

What might you do after a dizzy spell? ______

What might you do if you fall on your wrist?

______

6 Silly sentences. Use as many challenge words as possible to make a silly story.

______

______

______

______

Hard and soft c

1 Copy each list word.

act	______	mice	______	fence	______
ice	______	curl	______	slice	______
code	______	cent	______	space	______
clam	______	crash	______	scale	______
face	______	place	______	price	______
cube	______	dance	______	once	______
corn	______	twice	______		

2 Fill in the missing letters.

Ballet is a style of d___ ___c___.

The rocket flew into s___ ___c___.

A c___b___ has six faces.

Grandma cut me a s___ ___c___ of chocolate cake.

She had m___c___as her pets.

3 Unscramble it. Unscramble the letters to make the list word.

shrac	______	cie	______
eciwt	______	mlac	______
cta	______	paces	______
nfcee	______	lruc	______
nceo	______	cfea	______
nroc	______	deoc	______

Hard and soft c

Challenge words

4 Copy each challenge word.

fleece	__________	prince	__________
corner	__________	cattle	__________
juice	__________	crunch	__________
pencil	__________	chance	__________
coming	__________	circus	__________

5 Word clues. Which challenge word matches?

royalty __________

clowns, animals and acrobats __________

something you write with __________

an eating sound __________

something you can drink __________

animals that produce milk __________

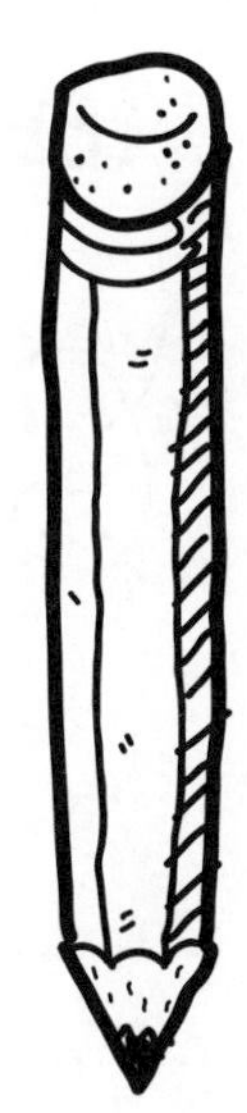

6 Choose it. Circle and rewrite the word to complete the sentence.

The [cattel] [cattle] ate a lot of grass. __________

We got the [fleece] [fleese] from a sheep. __________

There is a [chanse] [chance] it will rain. __________

I will be [coming] [comeing] to your party! __________

Vowel digraphs – ou and ow

1 Copy each list word.

bow ________	loud ________	proud ________
cow ________	sow ________	gown ________
our ________	noun ________	brown ________
now ________	cloud ________	sound ________
owl ________	count ________	clown ________
how ________	fowl ________	mouth ________
row ________	town ________	

2 Label it. Use a list word.

c ________ o ________ c ________ c ________

3 Sort the words.

ou		ow	

Vowel digraphs – ou and ow

Challenge words

4 Copy each challenge word.

mountain	______	couch	______
growl	______	frown	______
drown	______	flour	______
crowd	______	bound	______
found	______	about	______

5 Choose it. Circle and rewrite the correct word to complete the sentence.

We made the cake with [flower] [flour] . ______

I [found] [fonde] her behind the chair. ______

The [croud] [crowd] cheered loudly. ______

I [frowne] [frown] when I am sad. ______

My dogs [grole] [growl] at strangers. ______

I read [about] [aboot] China. ______

The [moundain] [mountain] is high. ______

6 Hidden words. Find the challenge word.

asdmountainln	______	adfaboutyeh	______
sdafloursyha	______	adercouchloq	______
asddrownasia	______	asdboundasiu	______

Word endings – et, it, ot

1 Copy each list word.

pocket	______	visit	______	rabbit	______
ticket	______	pilot	______	carrot	______
planet	______	helmet	______	puppet	______
jacket	______	goblet	______	bonnet	______
bucket	______	market	______	blanket	______
packet	______	carpet	______	basket	______
rocket	______	secret	______		

2 Circle the correct ending and rewrite the word.

pack	**et** / **ot**	______	rabb	**et** / **it**	______
pil	**et** / **ot**	______	secr	**et** / **it**	______
carr	**ot** / **et**	______	vis	**ot** / **it**	______

3 **Label it.** Use a list word.

h ______

b ______

p ______

r ______

Word endings – et, it, ot

Challenge words

4 Copy each challenge word.

tablet	______	comet	______
target	______	cricket	______
wallet	______	velvet	______
trumpet	______	violet	______
ferret	______	toilet	______

5 Complete the sentence.

He plays the ______ in the band.

The ______ flew through space.

The ______ had brown fur.

I keep money in my ______.

Our curtains are made of thick ______.

Dad reads a book on his computer ______.

6 Interesting question. Answer the question using a challenge word.

What can you flush? ______

What is a type of flower? ______

What do you shoot an arrow at? ______

What is an insect that makes a loud noise?

______

Vowel digraphs and trigraphs – or, ore

1 Copy each list word.

or	____	torn	____	torch	____
sore	____	fort	____	horse	____
more	____	port	____	chore	____
for	____	snore	____	acorn	____
corn	____	shore	____	store	____
fork	____	ashore	____	score	____
horn	____	before	____		

2 Fill in the words. Name the picture to complete the sentence.

We ate ____________ for dinner.

Jack rode a ____________ .

We took a trip to the sea ____________ .

She found a ____________ .

3 Unscramble it. Unscramble the letters to make a list word.

ropt	____	orme	____
ecohr	____	nsoer	____
osrec	____	hoaers	____
ro	____	rfo	____

Vowel digraphs and trigraphs – or, ore

Challenge words

4 Copy each challenge word.

adore	______	border	______
sport	______	force	______
storm	______	airport	______
afford	______	morning	______
corner	______	enormous	______

5 Solve it. Read the clue and complete the sentence.

Planes take off and land here. I am an ______.

You can play me. I am ______.

I am very large. I am ______.

I have thunder and lightning. I am a ______.

I happen before 12 pm. I am ______.

A triangle has three of me. I am a ______.

6 Hidden words. Find the challenge word.

pveadoregha ______

lheforceauk ______

cmtaffordqel ______

splborderanh ______

Suffixes – ing

1 Copy each list word.

ending ________	feeling ________	fetching ________
eating ________	wishing ________	reaching ________
sailing ________	locking ________	drinking ________
looking ________	going ________	speaking ________
saying ________	thinking ________	thanking ________
playing ________	speeding ________	floating ________
meeting ________	opening ________	

2 Label it. Use a list word.

d ________ p ________ f ________ e ________

3 Rainbow write. Write each list word in a different colour.

________ ________ ________

________ ________ ________

________ ________ ________

________ ________ ________

________ ________ ________

________ ________ ________

________ ________ ________

Suffixes – ing

Challenge words

4 Copy each challenge word.

blowing ______	wondering ______
brushing ______	gathering ______
tracking ______	watering ______
watching ______	smelling ______
covering ______	scratching ______

5 Hidden words. Find the challenge word.

fhitrackingysak ______

xetgatheringpvc ______

plrcoveringyij ______

ovtscratchingetcn ______

wbctwonderingeli ______

6 Choose it. Circle and rewrite the correct word to complete the sentence.

She was [smeling] [smelling] the roses. ______

The wind was [bloeing] [blowing] strongly. ______

Mum was [watering] [waterng] the plants. ______

My sister was [waching] [watching] TV. ______

He was [brushing] [brusing] the dog. ______

The storm clouds were [gathering] [gathring] in the sky.

______

Word endings – y

1 Copy each list word.

cry ______	tidy ______	sorry ______
sky ______	lazy ______	funny ______
fly ______	ugly ______	story ______
very ______	happy ______	party ______
copy ______	busy ______	city ______
body ______	easy ______	pretty ______
baby ______	puppy ______	

2 Name the picture.

p ______

c ______

b ______

c ______

h ______

s ______

3 **Unscramble it.** Unscramble the letters to make the list word.

nfuyn ______	zlay ______
yrev ______	tpyert ______
iydt ______	seay ______

Word endings – y

Challenge words

4 Copy each challenge word.

many	______	empty	______
fairy	______	angry	______
fancy	______	dirty	______
ready	______	clumsy	______
heavy	______	family	______

5 Solve it. Read the clue and complete the sentence with a list word.

It is not light. It is ______.

I am not full. I am ______.

I am covered in mud. I am ______.

The people related to you are your ______.

If I have a lot of something, I have ______.

I'm a magical creature with wings. I am a ______.

6 Silly sentences. Use as many challenge words as possible to make a silly story.

Vowel digraphs – oy and oi

1 Copy each list word.

oil ______	soil ______	ahoy ______
boy ______	join ______	oink ______
toy ______	moist ______	foil ______
joy ______	spoil ______	cowboy ______
noise ______	enjoy ______	royal ______
boil ______	oily ______	joyful ______
coin ______	point ______	

2 Correct it. Correct the misspelled word.

I really enjoi going to the beach. ______

The boi liked to run very fast. ______

I found a coyn in my pocket. ______

The coweboy wore a hat and boots. ______

3 Sort the words.

oy		oi	

Vowel digraphs – oy and oi

Challenge words

4 Copy each challenge word.

annoy ______	foyer ______
coy ______	avoid ______
coil ______	joint ______
destroy ______	toil ______
loyal ______	voice ______

5 Acrostic poem. Use the word **toil** to write an acrostic poem.

T ______

O ______

I ______

L ______

6 Choose it. Circle and rewrite the correct word to complete the sentence.

The snake lay in a [coyl] [coil] in the sun. ______

We waited in the hotel [foier] [foyer]. ______

She had a sweet singing [voice] [voyce]. ______

The dog was very [loyal] [loial]. ______

My elbow [joynt] [joint] was sore. ______

I'll leave early to [avoid] [avoyd] the rain. ______

Trigraphs – air, ear, are

1 Copy each list word.

air ____	pear ____	chair ____
ear ____	pair ____	share ____
fair ____	dear ____	stair ____
dare ____	care ____	spare ____
fear ____	near ____	smear ____
hair ____	year ____	spear ____
hear ____	wear ____	

2 Complete the word. Fill in the letters to make the list word.

c ___ ___ ___   y ___ ___ ___   a ___ ___

n ___ ___ ___   sh ___ ___ ___   sm ___ ___ ___

3 Label it.

c________   p________   h________   e________

4 Fill in the words.

She brushed her h__________.

I h__________ with my ears.

I d__________ you to tell the truth.

My puppy is d__________ to me.

Trigraphs – air, ear, are

Challenge words

5 Copy each challenge word.

beard	____________	weary	____________
scared	____________	nearby	____________
fairy	____________	square	____________
upstairs	____________	nightmare	____________
repair	____________	parent	____________

6 Interesting question. Answer the questions using a challenge word.

What is something you feel? ____________

What is a magical creature with wings? ____________

What is a name for a mother or father? ____________

What is the hair on a face? ____________

What is a four-sided shape? ____________

What do you call a bad dream? ____________

7 Acrostic poem. Write an acrostic poem using the word **beard**.

B ____________

E ____________

A ____________

R ____________

D ____________

Suffixes – ed

1 Copy each list word.

looked ______	played ______	cheated ______
wished ______	rushed ______	smiled ______
pulled ______	hired ______	roasted ______
rained ______	parked ______	blamed ______
cared ______	turned ______	washed ______
picked ______	shared ______	showed ______
cooked ______	choked ______	

2 Write the word in the brackets correctly.

I (pick) ______ it up yesterday.

Last time he (cheat) ______.

Dad (cook) ______ dinner last night.

She (choke) ______ trying to swallow the meat.

We (hire) ______ a jumping castle for my party.

Yesterday I (share) ______ my lunch with my friend

3 Addition words. Add the two parts to make the word.

wish	+	ed	=	
turn	+	ed	=	
look	+	ed	=	

Challenge words

4 Copy each challenge word.

called ____________ spilled ____________
freed ____________ crouched ____________
dressed ____________ grouped ____________
fetched ____________ stitched ____________
growled ____________ wondered ____________

5 Hidden words. Find the challenge word.

dfdressedasu ____________ tawonderedaj ____________
sscrouchedau ____________ plwfreedaid ____________
avstitchedaoi ____________ pcgroupedhg ____________

6 Choose it. Circle and rewrite the correct word to complete the sentence.

The dog [grouled] [growled] loudly at me. ____________
She [spilled] [spilet] her drink everywhere. ____________
I [called] [kalled] my grandma yesterday. ____________
I [croached] [crouched] down low. ____________
I [wundered] [wondered] what time we would arrive. ____________
I [grouped] [grooped] together the different types of shells. ____________

Word endings – le

1 Copy each list word.

able ______	little ______	jungle ______
uncle ______	bottle ______	cradle ______
candle ______	cuddle ______	juggle ______
apple ______	needle ______	purple ______
table ______	tickle ______	eagle ______
ankle ______	middle ______	bubble ______
kettle ______	chuckle ______	

2 Label it.

t ______

b ______

k ______

a ______

3 Rainbow write these list words.

able ______

purple ______

uncle ______

chuckle ______

middle ______

little ______

Word endings – le

Challenge words

4 Copy each challenge word.

castle ______________ freckle ______________
tremble ______________ struggle ______________
crumble ______________ circle ______________
startle ______________ bicycle ______________
sprinkle ______________ miracle ______________

5 Solve it. Read the clue and complete the sentence.

I am a large house where a king lives. I am a __________.

I have two wheels and a seat. I am a __________.

I am a shape with no corners. I am a __________.

I am a dot on the skin. I am a __________.

I am like a shiver. I am a __________.

I am an amazing event. I am a __________.

6 Silly sentence. Use as many challenge words as possible to make a silly story.

____

____

____

____

____

Vowel digraphs – ew and ue

1 Copy each list word.

dew ________	chew ________	due ________
blew ________	blue ________	threw ________
true ________	drew ________	grew ________
new ________	flew ________	screw ________
clue ________	crew ________	value ________
few ________	glue ________	knew ________
stew ________	pew ________	

2 Fill in the correct digraph.

bl ________	n ________
thr ________	kn ________
gl ________	bl ________

3 Write the list words in alphabetical order.

Vowel digraphs – ew and ue

Challenge words

4 Copy each challenge word.

venue	______	barbecue	______
nephew	______	Tuesday	______
avenue	______	rescue	______
pursue	______	jewel	______
cashew	______	argue	______

5 Interesting question. Answer the question using a challenge word.

What can you cook on? ______

What is another word for disagree? ______

What is a type of street? ______

6 Choose it. Circle and rewrite the correct word to complete the sentence.

The [jewll] [jewel] in her ring was green. ______

I am my aunt's [nephew] [nephue]. ______

I love to eat [cashue] [cashew] nuts. ______

[Tuesday] [Tuseday] is library day.

______

They plan to [rescue] [rescew] the hiker.

______

Consonant digraphs – wh, ph

1 Copy each list word.

why ______
what ______
when ______
where ______
wheel ______
white ______
which ______
while ______
whale ______
whip ______
whack ______
wheat ______
whirl ______
whisk ______
whine ______
phone ______
photo ______
nowhere ______
somewhere ______
anywhere ______

2 Label it.

p ______

w ______

p ______

w ______

3 Chunks. Put the list words back together.

ea–wh–t ______
i–ch–wh ______
ere–wh ______
ck–a–wh ______
i–wh–te ______
wh–an–ere–y ______
wh–no–ere ______
a–t–wh ______
y–wh ______
wh-so-er-me-e ______
e–n–wh ______
l–ir–wh ______

Challenge words

4 Copy each challenge word.

whisper	__________	nephew	__________
dolphin	__________	orphan	__________
phonics	__________	phew	__________
alphabet	__________	wharf	__________
elephant	__________	whether	__________

5 Solve it. Read the clue and complete the sentence.

I have a long trunk. I am an __________.

I have 26 letters. I am the __________.

I live in water and have a blowhole. I am a __________.

Boats and ships dock here. I am a __________.

I am someone who has no parents. I am an __________.

I am difficult to hear. I am a __________.

6 Hidden words. Find the challenge word.

weaphewauea __________

lemwhetherpqz __________

phonicsuebsky __________

tlenephewiah __________

Word endings – en, on

1 Copy each list word.

even ______	chicken ______	dragon ______
seven ______	children ______	wooden ______
oven ______	apron ______	cotton ______
garden ______	lesson ______	ribbon ______
lemon ______	sudden ______	button ______
wagon ______	golden ______	happen ______
open ______	kitten ______	

2 Addition words. Add the two parts to make the word.

lem	+	on	=	
op	+	en	=	
less	+	on	=	
chick	+	en	=	

3 Label it. Use a list word.

k ______

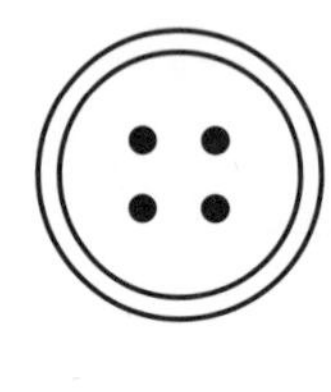

b ______

o ______

d ______

Word endings – en, on

Challenge words

4 Copy each challenge word.

person ______	eleven ______
season ______	onion ______
pardon ______	poison ______
bacon ______	carton ______
kitchen ______	listen ______

5 Interesting question. Answer each question using a challenge word.

What do you do with your ears? ______

Where do you cook? ______

What is the sum of ten and one? ______

What is summer? ______

What is a meat you often eat with eggs? ______

What is something that can harm or kill? ______

6 Silly sentence. Use as many challenge words as possible to make a silly story.

______

______

______

Vowel digraphs and trigraphs – ie, igh

1 Copy each list word.

die	______	dries	______	light	______
lie	______	spied	______	right	______
tie	______	fried	______	might	______
pie	______	thigh	______	sight	______
high	______	chief	______	fight	______
tries	______	thief	______	tight	______
cried	______	night	______		

2 Fill in the words. Complete the sentence using a list word.

The sun is h __ __ __ in the sky.

The bird s __ __ __ __ a worm on the ground.

The child c __ __ __ __ when he got hurt.

The c __ __ __ __ welcomed the visitors to his village.

I can t __ __ my shoelaces.

She cut me a piece of the p __ __ .

She d __ __ __ __ her face with a towel.

We had f __ __ __ __ chicken for lunch.

3 Unscramble these words.

iefth	______	ihgts	______
tghti	______	ghtri	______
iet	______	ihgth	______

Vowel digraphs and trigraphs – ie, igh

Challenge words

4 Copy each challenge word.

tonight	______	grief	______
bright	______	believe	______
flight	______	fright	______
slight	______	delight	______
belief	______	replies	______

5 Choose it. Circle and rewrite the correct word to complete the sentence.

The large dog gave me a [fright] [frite] . ______

The full moon was very [brite] [bright] . ______

She cried with [greef] [grief] . ______

Our [flight] [flite] to Hobart leaves soon. ______

6 Acrostic poem. Use the word **fright** to write an acrostic poem.

F ______

R ______

I ______

G ______

H ______

T ______

Suffixes – er, est

1 Copy each list word.

older	neatest	fresher
oldest	faster	freshest
longer	fastest	taller
longest	louder	tallest
later	loudest	shorter
latest	thicker	shortest
neater	thickest	

2 Sort the words.

er

est

3 **Chunks.** Rearrange the letters to make the list word.

est-st-fa	at-est-ne
ll-er-ta	ng-er-lo
rt-est-sho	sh-fr-er-e

Suffixes – er, est

Challenge words

4 Copy each challenge word.

quieter	____________	brightest	____________
quietest	____________	younger	____________
calmer	____________	youngest	____________
calmest	____________	higher	____________
brighter	____________	highest	____________

5 Complete the sentence.

My spelling score was ____________ than Toby's.

His motorcycle is ____________ than my dad's.

The sun shone the ____________ in the middle of the day.

6 Choose it. Circle and rewrite the correct word to complete the sentence.

The sea is calmer carmer today than yesterday. ____________

I climbed the higest highest tree. ____________

I am the youngest yungest of all my cousins. ____________

My bedroom is the quitest quietest place in our home. ____________

Vowel digraphs – au, aw

1 Copy each list word.

paw		lawn		dawn	
raw		hawk		haul	
saw		yawn		crawl	
jaw		straw		haunt	
law		thaw		fault	
claw		gawk		seesaw	
draw		shawl			

2 Name the picture.

s

p

d

h

3 Match the clue to a list word.

1.			r		
2.	l				
3.			w		
4.				k	
5.	s				
6.		h			
7.					l

1. dried grass
2. a rule
3. not cooked
4. stare
5. used to cut
6. melt
7. how a baby moves

Vowel digraphs – au, aw

Challenge words

4 Copy each challenge word.

awful	______	drawer	______
prawn	______	laundry	______
saucer	______	autumn	______
jigsaw	______	August	______
scrawl	______	author	______

5 Solve it. Read the clue and complete the sentence.

I am another name for a puzzle. I am a ______.

I write books. I am an ______.

I am messy writing. I am a ______.

You place me underneath a cup. I am a ______.

I slide in and out and hold items. I am a ______.

I am the season between summer and winter. I am ______.

6 Hidden words. Find the challenge word.

khYrAugustPfhj ______

ybvprawnhqt ______

lhqilaundryemfd ______

agvawfuloutn ______

slxyautumnkpst ______

Compound words

1 Copy each list word.

football ______

playground ______

farmyard ______

bedroom ______

handbag ______

strawberry ______

cupcake ______

bedtime ______

sunset ______

bullfrog ______

clockwork ______

baseball ______

popcorn ______

seaside ______

bathroom ______

sunshine ______

daydream ______

goldfish ______

weekend ______

postcard ______

2 Write the compound word.

\+ = ______

\+ = ______

\+ = ______

3 **Meaning.** Which list word means?

a small fish ______

a small red fruit ______

a game played with a bat and ball ______

to dream about something while awake ______

somewhere that children play ______

an animal that croaks ______

Compound words

Challenge words

4 Copy each challenge word.

footpath	____________	haircut	____________
jellyfish	____________	birthday	____________
sunflower	____________	someone	____________
grandson	____________	butterfly	____________
grandmother	____________	something	____________

5 Silly sentence. Use as many challenge words as possible to make a silly story.

____

____

____

____

____

6 Interesting question. Answer each question using a challenge word.

Who is your mother's mother? ____________

What is pretty and flies? ____________

Where do you walk? ____________

What do you have once a year? ____________

How do you get shorter hair? ____________

Tricky words

1 Copy each list word.

do ______	was ______	says ______
to ______	go ______	here ______
the ______	you ______	there ______
of ______	your ______	she ______
no ______	where ______	ask ______
by ______	they ______	were ______
are ______	said ______	

2 Sort the words.

2 letters

3 letters

4 letters

more than 4 letters

Challenge words

3 Copy each challenge word.

come	______	once	______
some	______	put	______
friend	______	push	______
school	______	pull	______
one	______	full	______

4 Choose it. Circle and rewrite the correct word to complete the sentence.

I've been to Disneyland [wonce] [once]. ______

Dad gave me a [push] [poosh] on the swing. ______

I was allowed [one] [won] scoop of ice-cream. ______

My [frend] [friend] and I are going to the park today. ______

5 Hidden words. Find the challenge word.

shlschoolkeb ______

stzfulluhb ______

lnbcomeplst ______

lhfputerx ______

lvesomehuq ______

Prefixes – un

1 Copy each list word.

undo ______	unfit ______	unwind ______
undid ______	unplug ______	unblock ______
untie ______	unpack ______	uneven ______
unzip ______	unable ______	untrue ______
unlock ______	undone ______	unroll ______
unlike ______	unwise ______	unsafe ______
unkind ______	untidy ______	

2 Chunks. Rearrange the letters to make the list word.

nd–un–ki ______	li–ke–un ______
le–ab–un ______	nd–un–wi ______
ck–un–lo ______	pa–ck–un ______
ug–pl–un ______	ev–un–en ______
ti–un–dy ______	sa–un–fe ______

3 Correct it. Correct the misspelled word.

The story she told you was unntru. ______

I had to unplugg the computer. ______

I helped untye her shoelaces. ______

It is unnsaf to swim in that river. ______

Challenge words

4 Copy each challenge word.

unwrap	________	unhappy	________
unfair	________	unusual	________
uncover	________	unclear	________
unlucky	________	unhealthy	________
unafraid	________	unfriendly	________

5 Silly sentence. Use as many challenge words as possible to make a silly story.

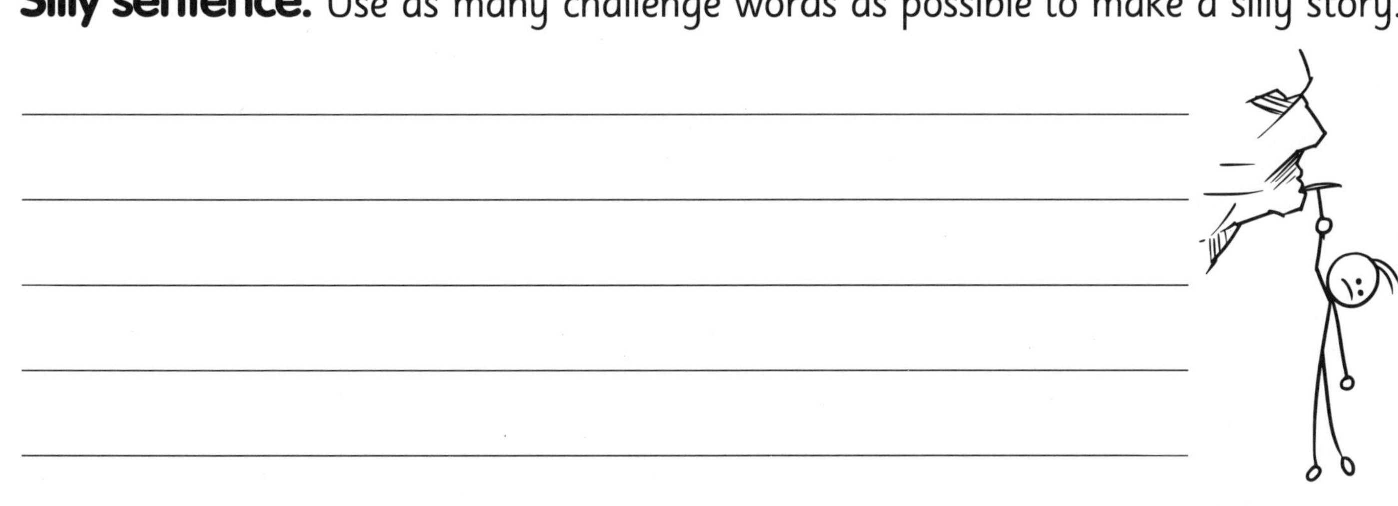

6 Solve it. Read the clue and complete the sentence.

You do this to a present. You ________ it.

When someone is sad they feel ________.

Too much junk food is ________.

Something surprising or interesting is ________.

When you feel brave you feel ________.

When something is confusing it is ________.

RULES AND GENERALISATIONS

Plurals

A plural is more than one. We use *s* and *es* to show plurals.

s, es	Adding *s* to a noun shows more than one, egg → *eggs*.
	For nouns that end in *s*, *sh, ch, x* and *z*, add *es*, peach → *peaches*.

Suffixes

A suffix is added to the end of a word to make a new word with a slightly different meaning.

ed	For past tense verbs just add *ed*, walk → *walked*.
	When the verb ends in *e*, just add *d*, share → *shared*.
ing	For many verbs just add *ing*.
	try → *trying* drink → *drinking* float → *floating*
er and *est*	To compare two nouns, add *er*, fresh → *fresher*.
	To compare MORE than two nouns, add *est*, loud → *loudest*.
	If it ends in *e*, just add *r* or *st*, brave → *braver* or *bravest*.